CW01239028

A Daily Devotional for *Daughters* of The King

Dr. Lisa Stewart

WestBow Press
A DIVISION OF THOMAS NELSON & ZONDERVAN

Copyright © 2024 Dr. Lisa Stewart.

All rights reserved. No part of this book may be used or reproduced by any means, graphic, electronic, or mechanical, including photocopying, recording, taping or by any information storage retrieval system without the written permission of the author except in the case of brief quotations embodied in critical articles and reviews.

WestBow Press books may be ordered through booksellers or by contacting:

WestBow Press
A Division of Thomas Nelson & Zondervan
1663 Liberty Drive
Bloomington, IN 47403
www.westbowpress.com
844-714-3454

Because of the dynamic nature of the Internet, any web addresses or links contained in this book may have changed since publication and may no longer be valid. The views expressed in this work are solely those of the author and do not necessarily reflect the views of the publisher, and the publisher hereby disclaims any responsibility for them.

Any people depicted in stock imagery provided by Getty Images are models, and such images are being used for illustrative purposes only. Certain stock imagery © Getty Images.

Interior Graphics/Art Credit: Lauren Arntz

ISBN: 979-8-3850-1771-3 (sc)
ISBN: 979-8-3850-1772-0 (hc)
ISBN: 979-8-3850-1917-5 (e)

Library of Congress Control Number: 2024902090

Print information available on the last page.

WestBow Press rev. date: 03/15/2024

Scripture quotations marked (KJV) are taken from
the King James Version, public domain.

Scripture quotations marked (NIV) are taken from the Holy Bible, NEW INTERNATIONAL VERSION®, NIV® Copyright © 1973, 1978, 1984, 2011 by Biblica, Inc.® Used by permission. All rights reserved worldwide.

Scripture quotations marked (ESV) are from the ESV® Bible (The Holy Bible, English Standard Version®), copyright © 2001 by Crossway, a publishing ministry of Good News Publishers. Used by permission. All rights reserved.

Scripture quotations marked (NASB) are taken from the NEW AMERICAN STANDARD BIBLE®, Copyright © 1960, 1962, 1963, 1968, 1971, 1972, 1973, 1975, 1977, 1995, 2020 by The Lockman Foundation. Used by permission.

Scripture quotations marked (CSB) have been taken from the Christian Standard Bible®, Copyright © 2017 by Holman Bible Publishers. Used by permission. Christian Standard Bible® and CSB® are federally registered trademarks of Holman Bible Publishers.

Scripture quotations marked (CEB) are from the Common English Bible (CEB) Copyright © 2011 by Common English Bible All rights reserved. Used by permission.(www.CommonEnglishBible.com).

DEDICATION

This book is dedicated to the special daughters
in my life, Trish, Laura, and Savannah!

CONTENTS

Chapter 1. Your Identity in Jesus Christ 1

   Day 1: You Are Forgiven 5
   Day 2: You Are a Child of God 7
   Day 3: You Are a Friend of Jesus Christ 9
   Day 4: You Are Chosen to Bear Fruit 11
   Day 5: You Are Justified 13
   Day 6: You Are a Joint Heir with Jesus Christ 15
   Day 7: You Are a Member of the Body of Christ 17
   Day 8: You Are a New Creation in Christ 19
   Day 9: You Are No Longer a Slave to Sin 21
   Day 10: You Are Redeemed 23
   Day 11: You Are Holy and Blameless 25
   Day 12: You Are Accepted by Jesus Christ 27
   Day 13: You Are God's Workmanship 29
   Day 14: You Are Seated in Heavenly Places 31
   Day 15: You Are a Citizen of Heaven 33

Chapter 2. Because you placed your faith in Jesus Christ ... 35

   Day 16: You Have Been Set Free 37
   Day 17: Your Old Self has been Crucified with Christ 39
   Day 18: You Have Not Been Condemned 41
   Day 19: You Have Been Called 43
   Day 20: You Have Been Given the Mind of Christ 45
   Day 21: You Have The Righteous of Christ Jesus 47
   Day 22: You Have the Blessings of God 49
   Day 23: You Have a New Family 51
   Day 24: You Have The Light of Christ 53
   Day 25: You Have a Provider 55
   Day 26: You Have Received The Holy Spirit 57
   Day 27: You Have The Peace of God 59
   Day 28: You Are Complete in Christ Jesus 61

Day 29: You Have Overcome the Enemy 63
Day 30: You Have Eternal Life 65

Chapter 3. Growing in Your Faith 67

Day 31: A Light to My Path 71
Day 32: Living By God's Word 73
Day 33: The Sword of The Spirit 75
Day 34: Study God's Word 77
Day 35: Hide the Word of God in My Heart 79
Day 36: Jesus Teaches Me How to Pray 85
Day 37: Pray and Confess My Sins 87
Day 38: Pray for My Enemies 89
Day 39: Pray Without Ceasing 91
Day 40: Give Thanks in All Things 93
Day 41: Meditate on God's Word 99
Day 42: Meditate Day and Night 101
Day 43: Meditate on These Things 103
Day 44: Meditate on God's Creation and Blessings 105
Day 45: Meditate on God's Precepts 107
Day 46: How We Should Fast 113
Day 47: A Biblical Illustration of Fasting - Moses 115
Day 48: A Biblical Illustration of Fasting - Esther 117
Day 49: A Biblical Illustration of Fasting - Daniel 119
Day 50: A Biblical Illustration of Fasting - Jesus 121
Day 51: A Time of Solitude – Find a Quiet Place 127
Day 52: A Time of Solitude –Use Your Time Wisely 129
Day 53: A Time of Solitude – Include a Time of Rest 131
Day 54: A Time of Solitude – Expect to Meet God 133
Day 55: A Time of Solitude – Time to Talk to God 135
Day 56: Lift Your Hands in Worship to the Lord 141
Day 57: Worship Our Great God 143
Day 58: Worship and Bow Down Before the Lord 145
Day 59: A Call to Praise and Worship 147
Day 60: Join With the Angels and Worship God 149

CHAPTER 1

YOUR IDENTITY IN JESUS CHRIST

As you prepare to read this devotional, you may ask yourself "Am I a daughter of the King", "Am I a child of God"? If the answer is no or I'm not sure, below are the steps you can follow to become a Christian, a child of God!

1. **Admit you are a sinner and recognize your need for a Savior.** Why is this necessary? The Bible says in Romans 3:23, *"All have sinned and come short of the glory of God"* (KJV). Romans 3:10 says, *"As it is written, there is none righteous, no, not one"* (KJV). That means we all are sinners and all the good we do cannot produce the righteousness needed to save us.

2. **Believe that Jesus Christ died on the cross to pay your sin debt.** The Bible says in Romans 6:23, *"The wages of sin is death, but the gift of God is eternal life through Jesus Christ our Lord" (KJV).* Romans 5:8 says, *"But God shows his love for us in that while we were still sinners, Christ died for us."* (ESV) God, the King of Kings, knew we could not pay this debt and He loves us so much that He sent His son, Jesus Christ, to pay the penalty of our sin debt. Jesus loved us so much that He took our place and willingly suffered on the cross to pay for our sins. There is nothing you can ever do to pay the penalty for your sins!

3. **Confess your sins to God in prayer.** As you pray, tell God you know that you are a sinner and ask him to forgive you of your sins. Tell him that you believe Jesus paid for your sins by dying on the cross in your place. Ask Jesus to come into your heart and lead you from this day forward.

Below is a prayer that you can pray. Remember, it's not the prayer that saves you, but your belief in the finished work of Jesus Christ on Calvary's cross!

Prayer of Salvation

Dear Heavenly Father, I know that I'm a sinner and my sin separates me from you. Forgive me of my sins and cleanse me of my unrighteousness. I believe that Jesus Christ died on the cross to pay for my sins. Come into my heart, Jesus, and lead me from this day forward. Thank you for being my Savior and now the Lord of my life. In Jesus name, Amen.

Daughter

OF THE KING ...

DAY 1

YOU ARE FORGIVEN

*If we confess our sins, he is faithful and just to forgive us
our sins and to cleanse us from all unrighteousness.*
—1 John 1:9 (KJV)

Are there days when you feel like a failure, doubt your salvation, or still struggle wondering if God has truly forgiven you of your sins? Your struggle is real because the enemy wants you to be fearful and doubtful of your salvation. He wants you to see yourself as a failure not worthy of forgiveness. Remember Jesus's death on the cross paid the penalty of your sins once and for all.

If you are still struggling with a lingering sin, remember, First John 1:9 (KJV) says, "If we confess our sins, He (God) is faithful to forgive us of our sins and cleanse us from all unrighteousness." When I think of this verse, I liken it to the Christian's bar of soap, which means we have to use it daily. Not only will God forgive us and cleanse us of our sins, but Psalm 103 says that God will also cast our sins as far as the east is from the west. Just as the east and west never meet, God will never remind you of your sins. So trust God at His Word, and receive His forgiving grace that He offers so freely!

Dear Heavenly Father,

Thank you for forgiving me of my sins as I confess them to you. Thank you for never reminding me of my sins and for removing them as far as the East is from the West. I receive your forgiveness today, and I trust you always! Amen!

Daughter
OF THE KING ...

DAY 2

YOU ARE A CHILD OF GOD

> But to all who did receive him, who believed in his name, he gave the right to become children of God.
> —John 1:12 (ESV)

When you placed your faith in Jesus Christ, not only were you forgiven of your sins, but you were also given a new identity as a child of God. This right isn't given to just everyone. John 1:12 reminds us that for everyone who receives Jesus Christ as Savior and believes in His name, God gave us the right to become sons and daughters of God. Have you received Jesus Christ as Savior? Do you believe in the name of Jesus? If so, as you go throughout this day, remember who you are and remember whose you are. You are a child of God; you are a daughter of the King of Kings!

Dear Heavenly Father,
    Thank you for loving me so much that you would call me your child. I recognize this honor is not given to everyone, and I am honored to be called your child and recognized as a daughter of the King. Amen!

Daughter
OF THE KING ...

DAY 3

YOU ARE A FRIEND OF JESUS CHRIST

No longer do I call you servants, for the servant does not know what his master is doing; but I have called you friends, for all that I have heard from my Father I have made known to you.
—John 15:15 (ESV)

"What a Friend We Have in Jesus" is a Christian hymn written by Preacher Joseph M. Scriven as a poem in 1855. The lyrics of this song are a reminder that you can take all of your sins, burdens, problems, cares, and concerns to Jesus. Why? Because He is a faithful friend who will love you and will bear your burdens. John 15:15 should always be a reminder to you that Jesus calls you His friend and He will make known to you all that the Father has shared with Him!

Dear Heavenly Father,

What a joy and a privilege to be called a friend of Jesus Christ! Thank you that I can bring all my worries, cares, and concerns to you in prayer because you are my faithful friend and burden bearer. Amen.

Daughter
OF THE KING ...

DAY 4

YOU ARE CHOSEN TO BEAR FRUIT

> You did not choose Me but I chose you, and appointed you that you would go and bear fruit, and that your fruit would remain, so that whatever you ask of the Father in My name He may give to you.
> —John 15:16 (NASB)

As believers, you were chosen and saved to bear fruit. The type of fruit believers bear will remain throughout eternity, which is the salvation of the souls of those who don't know Jesus Christ as Savior. Jesus died to pay the penalty of sin for all humankind; therefore, it is important for you to share the message of salvation to those who are lost. Are you bearing fruit by sharing the gospel? If the answer is no, it is not too late to start!

Dear Heavenly Father,

Thank you for choosing me to bear fruit. Help me to be a good steward of the souls you have entrusted to me by sharing the Gospel message with those who are lost. Amen!

Daughter
OF THE KING ...

DAY 5

YOU ARE JUSTIFIED

> We are justified by his grace as a gift, through
> the redemption that is in Christ Jesus.
> —Romans 3:24 (ESV)

When you placed your faith in Jesus Christ, God declared you to be righteous before Him! Jesus paid your sin debt on Cavalry's cross by shedding His own sinless blood. As a result, your dark sins have been washed white, and as a Christian, you are now justified by God. Justification does not mean that God sees you as having never sinned. God sees you as having the righteousness of Jesus applied as the redemptive price for your sins. God extended His grace by pardoning the sins of believers through the sacrifice of His Son, Jesus Christ, who took our place and died for our sins.

Dear Heavenly Father,
    Thank you for the grace of justification you have provided through the redemptive work of Jesus Christ. Amen!

Daughter
OF THE KING ...

DAY 6

YOU ARE A JOINT HEIR WITH JESUS CHRIST

> And if children, then heirs; heirs of God and fellow heirs with Christ.
> —Romans 8:17 (ESV)

When an earthly parent prepares their will, they leave an inheritance to their children. God the Father has transferred the inheritance of the universe to His Son, Jesus Christ, and as a joint heir with Jesus, you share in His inheritance. Our Heavenly Father has entrusted everything to Jesus. The inheritance believers will receive is glorified bodies when we come into the kingdom of God. Your identity as a daughter of the King makes you a joint heir with Jesus Christ!

Dear Heavenly Father,

Thank you for the joy of being a joint heir with Jesus, allowing me to share in the inheritance you have entrusted to him. Amen!

Daughter
OF THE KING ...

DAY 7

YOU ARE A MEMBER OF THE BODY OF CHRIST

For just as the body is one and has many members, and all the members of the body, though many, are one body, so it is with Christ. For in one Spirit we were all baptized into one body Jews or Greeks, slaves or free and all were made to drink of one Spirit.
—1 Corinthians 12:12–13 (ESV)

We know our human bodies have different parts (members): our head, hands, eyes, legs, feet, etc. Just as the body has many members, the church, which is the body of Christ, also has many members. As a believer, you are a member of the body of Christ. As a member of this growing and diverse body, you can be the hands and feet of Jesus Christ using your spiritual gifts to serve within your local church and your community.

Dear Heavenly Father,
   I am so excited to be a member of the body of Christ. Show me how to use my gifts to be the hands and feet of Jesus in my church, workplace, and community to serve you and to serve others. Amen!

Daughter

OF THE KING ...

DAY 8

YOU ARE A NEW CREATION IN CHRIST

> Therefore, if anyone is in Christ, he is a new creation.
> The old has passed away; behold, the new has come.
> —2 Corinthians 5:17 (ESV)

Everyone is born of "a natural birth" and born in sin, but when we are "born again," we become a new creation in Christ Jesus! That means the old way of living is gone. My family enjoys fishing a lot. Our daughter, six years old at the time, never wanted to get out of the car because she was fearful of being near the water. She was seven years old when she prayed to receive Christ as Savior. After she was saved, we noticed the next time we went fishing, she was the first one out of the car and was no longer fearful of the water. We witnessed 2 Corinthians 5:17 lived out in our daughter's life as she demonstrated the old fearful life was gone and she was now a new creation in Christ Jesus. What are you still struggling with that has you in bondage? Don't continue living your old way of life. Celebrate the new life you have in Christ Jesus.

Dear Heavenly Father,
    Thank you for the gift of salvation allowing me to be a new creation in Christ Jesus. I'm thankful my old way of living is gone and I can live my new life through you! Amen.

Daughter

OF THE KING ...

DAY 9

YOU ARE NO LONGER A SLAVE TO SIN

> Therefore, you are no longer a slave but a son or daughter, and if you are his child, then you are also an heir through God.
> —Galatians 4:7 (CEB)

As believers, we wrestle daily with our sinful nature. Galatians 4:7 reminds us that we are no longer slaves to sin. Jesus Christ paid the price owed for our sins. His death delivered us from slavery and we are members of God's family. What does this mean for you? You dear sister have been adopted as a daughter of God and an heir through Jesus Christ. As a daughter of God, you can call out to Him, Abba, which is interpreted as Father, because He is your Heavenly Father. Remember you are no longer a slave, but a daughter of the King.

Dear Heavenly Father,

Thank you for delivering me from the bondage of being a slave to sin and adopting me as your child. Show me how to turn away from the desire to live in the past and to walk in obedience to your word as a daughter of the King! Amen.

Daughter
OF THE KING ...

DAY 10

YOU ARE REDEEMED

"In Him, we have redemption through his blood, the forgiveness of our trespasses, according to the riches of his grace."
—Ephesians 1:7(ESV)

Fanny Crosby wrote the popular hymn **Redeemed by the Blood of the Lamb.** The biblical definition of redeemed means saved or delivered from sin. The blood of Jesus Christ, the lamb of God, provided redemption for your sins when He took your place on the cross, paying the price for your sin debt. Because you have placed your faith in Jesus, you have complete forgiveness of your sin by the grace of God!

Dear Heavenly Father,
    Thank you for saving me and providing redemption through the blood of Jesus Christ for my sins. I acknowledge that there was nothing I could do to save myself. It is by grace that I have been saved, through my faith in the finished work of Jesus Christ. Amen.

Daughter

OF THE KING ...

DAY 11

YOU ARE HOLY AND BLAMELESS

> Even as he chose us in him before the foundation of the world, that we should be holy and blameless before him.
> —Ephesians 1:4 (ESV)

Whether you are a new or mature Christian, you may struggle with understanding how to live a life that is holy and blameless before God. You must begin by understanding the first part of Ephesians 1:4, which is "***You have been chosen***". Because God chose you before the foundation of the world to live a holy and blameless life He will equip you to do so. Living a holy life requires committing your heart to the Lord and allowing Him to transfer your unclean heart to one that is blameless in holiness. Living a blameless life before the Holy God requires denying oneself, trusting God completely, and living a life guided by faith in God.

Dear Heavenly Father,

I want to live my life holy and blameless before you. I commit my heart to You and I trust You to guide me daily in every area of my life as I walk by faith following You. Amen.

Daughter

OF THE KING ...

DAY 12

YOU ARE ACCEPTED BY JESUS CHRIST

> To the praise of the glory of his grace, wherein
> he hath made us accepted in the beloved.
> —Ephesians 1:6 (KJV)

What does it mean to be accepted by Jesus Christ? As a believer, you are accepted because you placed your faith in Jesus Christ trusting Him as your Savior and Lord of your life. This acceptance also confirms your adoption by God into His family. You don't have to fill out an application, there is nothing you can do to earn this acceptance. Daughter of God, you are accepted by God because He loves you and because you trust in Jesus. So walk by faith and with your head held high knowing that you are accepted in the beloved.

Dear Heavenly Father,

Thank you for loving me and accepting me into Your family even though I didn't deserve it. By your grace, you extended mercy and accepted me into the beloved. Thank you so much. Amen

Daughter
OF THE KING ...

DAY 13

YOU ARE GOD'S WORKMANSHIP

> For we are his workmanship, created in Christ
> Jesus for good works, which God prepared
> beforehand, that we should walk in them.
> —Ephesians 2:10 (ESV)

Two common questions many believers have is "What is my purpose? And "Why am I here?" The answer is found in Ephesians 2:10, we were created in Christ Jesus to do good works. Do not make the mistake of thinking that doing good works is a requirement for salvation because it is not. We are saved by grace and not by works. God has skillfully designed you with unique gifts, talents, and abilities to do the work He has equipped you to do. As His child, your good works are seen as fruits of salvation, because the work of every believer is to bear fruit of living out the great commission, which is to make disciples.

Dear Heavenly Father,

Thank you for equipping me with the gifts, talents, and ability to do the work of making disciples. Bless the work of my hands as I seek to bear the fruit of salvation by sharing the Gospel with those who are lost. Amen.

Daughter
OF THE KING ...

DAY 14

YOU ARE SEATED IN HEAVENLY PLACES

Even when we were dead in our trespasses, made us alive together with Christ by grace you have been saved and raised us up with him and seated us with him in the heavenly places in Christ Jesus.
—Ephesians 2:5-6 (ESV)

Before you were saved, you were dead in your sin. When you were saved you became a child of God made alive with Jesus Christ. God has seated you positionally in Heaven, not because of anything you have done, but because of Jesus Christ. At the point of your salvation, God transformed your identity as a child of God. He made you a new creation and now daughter of God, you are seated in heavenly places in Jesus Christ!

Dear Heavenly Father,
 Thank you for my new identity as your child. Thank you that you have seated me positionally in Heaven by your grace and the finished work of Jesus Christ. Amen.

Daughter
OF THE KING ...

DAY 15

YOU ARE A CITIZEN OF HEAVEN

> But our citizenship is in heaven, and from it,
> we await a Savior, the Lord Jesus Christ.
> —Philippian 3:20 (ESV)

Philippians 3:20 provides instructions to not focus on the things of the world. Instead, the focus should be on Christ and His return because this is pleasing to God. As a child of God, your citizenship is in Heaven. This means while living on earth, you should remember this is not your home. You should not focus on the things of this world. You should not focus on your former life, instead, you should focus on building up the kingdom of God!

Dear Heavenly Father,

I am thankful to be your child and to know my citizenship is in Heaven. I am committed to focusing on the return of Christ and all that is pleasing to you. Amen

Daughter
OF THE KING ...

CHAPTER 2

BECAUSE YOU PLACED YOUR FAITH IN JESUS CHRIST

Before placing faith in Jesus Christ, you recognize you are a sinner and your sin separated you from God. You also became aware that you could not pay the penalty for your sins, which the Bible says the penalty is death. Because of God's love for all mankind, He sent his Son Jesus Christ to pay your sin debt. Jesus willingly laid down His life and died on the cross as payment for your sin debt. The day you placed your faith in Jesus Christ, you became a child of God. As His daughter, you can receive the blessings God has made available to all who receive Jesus Christ as Savior, to those who believe in His name. This next section of the devotional will share some of the blessings God has made available for you!

Daughter
OF THE KING ...

DAY 16

YOU HAVE BEEN SET FREE

> So, if the Son sets you free, you will be free indeed.
> —John 8:36 (ESV)

When a prisoner is released from prison they are free from the bondage of prison life. But many have to report regularly to their parole officer, so it's not complete freedom. John 8:36 says if the son sets you free, you are free indeed. Because Jesus Christ paid our sin debt, you have been set free from the law of sin and death. This means you can live free from the law of sin and death and live in the righteousness of God.

Dear Heavenly Father,

Thank you for the freedom I now have as a child of God! Jesus, thank you for taking my place and paying my sin debt. I choose to live in the freedom you have made available to me. Amen.

Daughter
OF THE KING ...

DAY 17

YOUR OLD SELF HAS BEEN CRUCIFIED WITH CHRIST

> I am crucified with Christ: nevertheless, I live; yet not I, but Christ liveth in me: and the life which I now live in the flesh I live by the faith of the Son of God, who loved me, and gave himself for me.
> —Galatians 2:20 (KJV)

When you place your faith in Jesus Christ, your old self was crucified with Jesus on Calvary's cross. As a new creation in Christ Jesus, you recognize you are not perfect because you still live in a mortal body and can sin. As a Christian, you don't live the way you did before. When you sin, you seek God's forgiveness, you put away the old way of thinking, the old way of doing things your own way, and you trust Christ completely with your life. Because Jesus Christ died for your sins, you can live with the assurance that you have been crucified with Christ and that He lives in you. The life you now live in the body you live by faith in Jesus Christ, who loves you and gave Himself for you.

Dear Heavenly Father,
    Thank you that my old self has been crucified with Christ and that I can live by faith in Jesus Christ who gave His life for me to pay for my sins. I commit to following as you lead and guide me each day. Amen.

Daughter

OF THE KING ...

DAY 18

YOU HAVE NOT BEEN CONDEMNED

> There is therefore now no condemnation to them which are in Christ Jesus, who walk not after the flesh, but after the Spirit.
> —Romans 8:1 (KJV)

When a person is guilty of a crime, they are condemned (sentenced) and punished by law. The penalty for sin is death. As a Christian, you are not condemned for your sins because you are not under the law. Jesus's death covered your sins and freed you from the penalty of death. Satan will try to remind you of your past and of your sins, attempting to bring you under condemnation. When that happens, just remind Satan that he has no authority in your life because Jesus has all authority in your life.

Dear Heavenly Father,

Thank you for the reminder in your Word that there is no condemnation to those who are in Jesus Christ. Thank you that my sins have been covered by the blood of Jesus Christ and I have been set free from the penalty of death because I placed my faith in Jesus Christ! Amen.

Daughter
OF THE KING ...

DAY 19

YOU HAVE BEEN CALLED

> ...to those sanctified in Christ Jesus and called to be his holy people, together with all those everywhere who call on the name of our Lord Jesus Christ, their Lord and ours.
> —First Corinthians 1:2 (NIV)

The primary call for believers is threefold. First, you have been called to salvation through your personal relationship with God by faith in Jesus Christ. Second, you have been called to sanctification, which is to be set apart for His purpose, which is to act justly, love mercy, and walk humbly with him. (Micah 6:8). Third, you are called to serve by carrying out God's work and fulfilling the Great Commission. Because Jesus Christ paid the penalty for your sins and you have placed your faith in Him, you are encouraged to remember the reasons you have been called and to serve in a manner that fulfills your calling.

Dear Heavenly Father,

Thank you for reminding me that I have been called and set apart for the specific purpose you have for my life. Show me each day how to carry out your work, to act justly, to love mercy and to walk humbly with you as I commit to fulfilling the Great Commission of making disciples! Amen.

Daughter
OF THE KING ...

DAY 20

YOU HAVE BEEN GIVEN THE MIND OF CHRIST

> For who has known the mind of the Lord, that he will instruct him? But we have the mind of Christ.
> —First Corinthians 2:16 (NASB)

When you were born again, you were given the mind of Jesus Christ, which enables you to discern spiritual things. As you study and meditate on God's Word, your mind is constantly being renewed, which will help you discern God's will for your life. With the mind of Christ, you can think about things that are true, honorable, right, pure, loving, and commendable. (Philippians 4:8) As the daughter of God, you are encouraged to keep your mind fixed on Jesus!

Dear Heavenly Father,

Thank you for your Word, which reminds and instructs me in the way I should live and what I should think about. Help me each day to keep my mind on Jesus and think about things that align with Your Word. Amen.

Daughter
OF THE KING ...

DAY 21

YOU HAVE THE RIGHTEOUS OF CHRIST JESUS

He made Him who knew no sin to be sin in our behalf so that we might become the righteousness of God in Him.
—Second Corinthians 5:21 (NASB)

2 Corinthians 5:21 is a reminder that Jesus Christ, the spotless lamb of God, was the perfect sacrifice to pay for your sins. He was perfect because He was without sin. However, He became sin for you by laying down his life and taking the punishment for your sins. He paid your sin debt with His life. With your new identity as a child of God, you now have the righteousness of Christ. That means when God looks at you, He does not see your sin. He sees the perfect righteousness of his Son Jesus Christ!

Dear Heavenly Father,

Thank you for loving me so much that you would allow your son to be the sacrifice to pay for my sins. What a joy in knowing that when you look at me you no longer see my sin, but you see the perfect righteousness of your Son, Jesus Christ in my life. Amen.

Daughter
OF THE KING ...

DAY 22

YOU HAVE THE BLESSINGS OF GOD

> Blessed be the God and Father of our Lord Jesus Christ, who has blessed us with every spiritual blessing in the heavenly places in Christ.
> —Ephesians 1:3 (NASB)

As a daughter of the king, when you were saved, your Heavenly Father blessed you with every spiritual blessing you need for life and godliness. You have the blessing of salvation, the Holy Spirit, adoption into the family of God, redemption by the blood of Jesus Christ, eternal life, and so much more. Today, daughter of God, you are encouraged to live your life in the fullness of knowing that you have truly been blessed by God.

Dear Heavenly Father,

Thank you for all the many blessings that you have given to me. I am truly humbled to know how much you love me and how much you have given to me because I am your child and because I have placed my faith in Jesus Christ. I love you so much and I am thankful that you are my Heavenly Father. Amen.

Daughter
OF THE KING ...

DAY 23

YOU HAVE A NEW FAMILY

So, then you are no longer strangers and foreigners, but you are fellow citizens with the saints, and are of God's household.
—Ephesians 2:19 (NASB)

Ephesians 2:19 is a reminder that you are not a foreigner or a nonresident with no rights or a stranger with limited rights. When you placed your faith in Jesus Christ, you not only became a Christian but you were adopted into God's family. You don't need to apply for citizenship. As a member of the family of God, you are a citizen of heaven with full rights and privileges. As a member of God's family, you have more brothers and sisters, than you can count, who are also believers in Christ and you can meet with them regularly in a Bible believing, Bible teaching, church, and fellowship together.

Dear Heavenly Father,
    I could never thank you enough for adopting me into your family and calling me Your child. Thank you for reminding me that as your child I have other brothers and sisters who are also Christians that I can fellowship with as we grow together in our faith in Jesus Christ. Amen.

Daughter

OF THE KING ...

DAY 24

YOU HAVE THE LIGHT OF CHRIST

> For you were once darkness, but now you are
> light in the Lord; walk as children of light.
> —Ephesians 5:8 (NASB)

Before you were saved, your life was full of sin and darkness. But when you place your faith in Jesus Christ you now have the light of Christ. This means your life should always reflect the goodness and grace of Jesus Christ. When others look at you, they should see you living out the truth of God's Word obediently. So daughter of God, walk as a child of the light of Jesus Christ.

Dear Heavenly Father,

Help me today to walk not only as a child of God, but to reflect the light of Jesus Christ. Hide me behind the cross, so when others see me, they see You in my life! Amen.

Daughter
OF THE KING ...

DAY 25

YOU HAVE A PROVIDER

> And my God will supply all your needs according
> to His riches in glory in Christ Jesus.
> —Philippians 4:19 (CSB)

As you read Philippians 4:19, let it be a reminder to you that Jehovah Jireh, the Lord is your provider. He knows your needs even before you ask Him. Many of us have a long list of wants, things that we desire but are not necessarily what we need. But God knows what is best for us, which is why He will provide your needs and not your wants. As believers, we are to be good stewards of everything God has blessed us with.

Dear Heavenly Father,
    Thank you for meeting and providing for all my needs. I am so thankful that you know what is best for me and that you don't give me everything that I want. I want your perfect will for my life. Help me each day to be a good steward of all that you have blessed me with. Amen!

Daughter

of The King ...

DAY 26

YOU HAVE RECEIVED THE HOLY SPIRIT

> In Him, you also, after listening to the message of truth, the gospel of your salvation having also believed, you were sealed in Him with the Holy Spirit of the promise.
> —Ephesians 1:13 (NASB)

The moment you place your faith in Jesus Christ, you receive the Holy Spirit. The Holy Spirit is the third member of the Trinity. The role of the Holy Spirit is to be your helper, helping you to understand God's Word as you read and study it; to be your comforter during times of stress and anxiety; to be your guide, as He leads you and guides you to all truth; to be your counselor teaching and encouraging you to walk in the way of the Lord. The Holy Spirit is also the giver of spiritual gifts that you will use as you serve the Lord and others. Be assured that the Holy Spirit will never lead you into sin. So trust the Holy Spirit to lead you each and every day.

Dear Heavenly Father,
    Teach me to walk in the Spirit by yielding my life to full control of the Holy Spirit, so that I may produce and bear the fruit of the Spirit in my life.

Daughter
OF THE KING ...

DAY 27

YOU HAVE THE PEACE OF GOD

> And the peace of God, which surpasses all comprehension,
> will guard your hearts and minds in Christ Jesus.
> —Philippians 4:7 (NASB)

On occasion, many people struggle with worrying. They worry about health issues, finances, children, job issues, and many other things. Peace is something that everyone desires, whether it's in their individual life, within their family, their homes, their marriages, etc. If you want peace, you can seek peace from the giver of peace, Jesus Christ. As believers, Philippians 4:7 reminds us that we don't need to worry because when we present our requests to the Lord, He will provide peace beyond our understanding that will not only bless us but will remove our fears and calm our anxiety.

Dear Heavenly Father,
   Forgive me for worrying instead of trusting you. Thank you for reminding me that you are the peace giver. So I place all my cares on you and I trust you to bring peace in the situation that I'm facing. Amen.

Daughter
OF THE KING ...

DAY 28

YOU ARE COMPLETE IN CHRIST JESUS

> "His divine power has granted to us everything pertaining to life and godliness."
> —Second Peter 1:3 (NASB)

What does it mean to be complete in Christ? It means to have what you need as a believer, a child of God, to live your life in full obedience to God. Second Peter 1:3 is a great reminder that God has provided believers everything required for life and godliness. Believers have the promise of eternal life and wisdom and knowledge are available in God's Word on how to live our life here on earth in a godly and Christ-like manner daily. The Bible tells us to seek and we shall find (Matthew 4;7-8) to study and show ourselves approved to God. (2 Timothy 2:15) Daughter of God, you are encouraged to have regular study time in God's Word and when you do, you will have the assurance of knowing you have received everything you need to be complete in Christ Jesus!

Dear Heavenly Father,
    Thank you for reminding me that you have given me everything I need pertaining to life and godliness. Help me each day to read and study your word, to apply it to my life, so I can live in true obedience to You. Amen.

Daughter
of The King ...

DAY 29

YOU HAVE OVERCOME THE ENEMY

> And they overcame him because of the blood of the Lamb and because of the word of their testimony, and they did not love their life even when faced with death.
> —Revelations 12:11 (NASB)

As a believer, you are constantly in a spiritual battle. Satan, your enemy, will stop at nothing to try and trip you up and keep you from being faithful in your walk with Christ. Revelations 12:11 is a reminder that you can overcome the enemy because of your faith in Jesus Christ. The key to being an overcomer is to not give up or give in to the temptations of the enemy. Remember, you have spiritual armor that you can put on each day to help equip you for spiritual battle. While suited in the armor of God, remember you are not in the battle alone because the Lord promised he will never leave or forsake you!

Dear Heavenly Father,

Thank you for providing spiritual armor that I can put on each day to equip me for the spiritual battles I will face in life. Thank you for reminding me that I don't have to face these battles alone because you are with me. Because you are with me, I am an overcomer! Amen

Daughter
OF THE KING ...

DAY 30

YOU HAVE ETERNAL LIFE

For God so loved the world, that He gave His only Son, so that everyone who believes in Him will not perish but have eternal life. For God did not send the Son into the world to judge the world, but so that the world might be saved through Him.
—John 3:16-17 (NASB)

John 3:16 is the most popular scripture in the Bible and provides the foundation of God's plan of redemption for mankind. Though we were born in sin, God loved us so much that He sent his Son Jesus Christ into the world to pay the penalty of our sin debt. He did not send His son to condemn you, but to save you. Daughter of God, when you placed your faith in Jesus Christ, you were given the gift of eternal life. The promise of eternal life means life does not end after death for believers. You will spend eternity in heaven!

Dear Heavenly Father,

Thank you so much for your love for me. You not only saved me when I placed my faith in Jesus, but you also gave me the promise of eternal life. I know I will spend eternity in Heaven with You! Amen

CHAPTER 3

GROWING IN YOUR FAITH

Now that you know your identity in Christ as the daughter of the King, and you are aware of the blessings available to you as a child of God, you need to grow in your Christian faith. Spiritual growth is achieved as you apply the spiritual discipline to your life.

This section of the devotional includes a daily devotion related to the spiritual disciplines which are Scripture Reading, Prayer, Meditation, Fasting, Solitude, and Worship.

Each devotional message includes a scripture verse to read, related to the spiritual discipline, a devotional message, a prayer, and a commitment page for you to share how you will apply each discipline to your life.

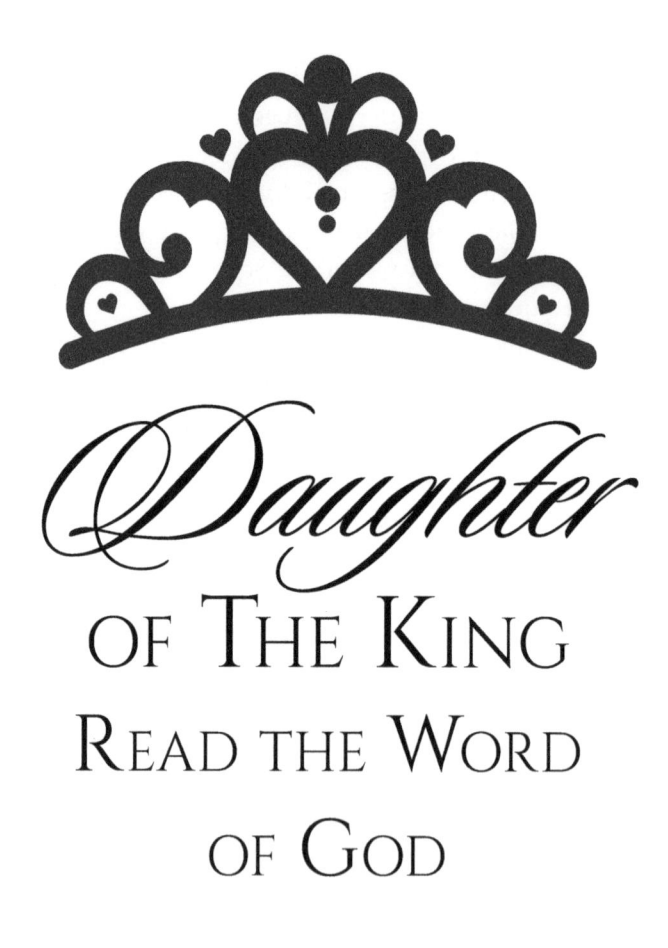

Daughter
OF THE KING
READ THE WORD OF GOD

THE SPIRITUAL DISCIPLINE OF READING THE WORD OF GOD

The Bible, God's Word, is often referred to as a letter to His children. The spiritual discipline of reading God's Word is to assist believers in growing in their faith as they read, study, and memorize scriptures. Second Timothy 3:16-17 says, "All Scripture is inspired by God and beneficial for teaching, for rebuke, for correction, for training in righteousness; so that the man or woman of God may be fully capable, equipped for every good work." (NASB)

Daughter

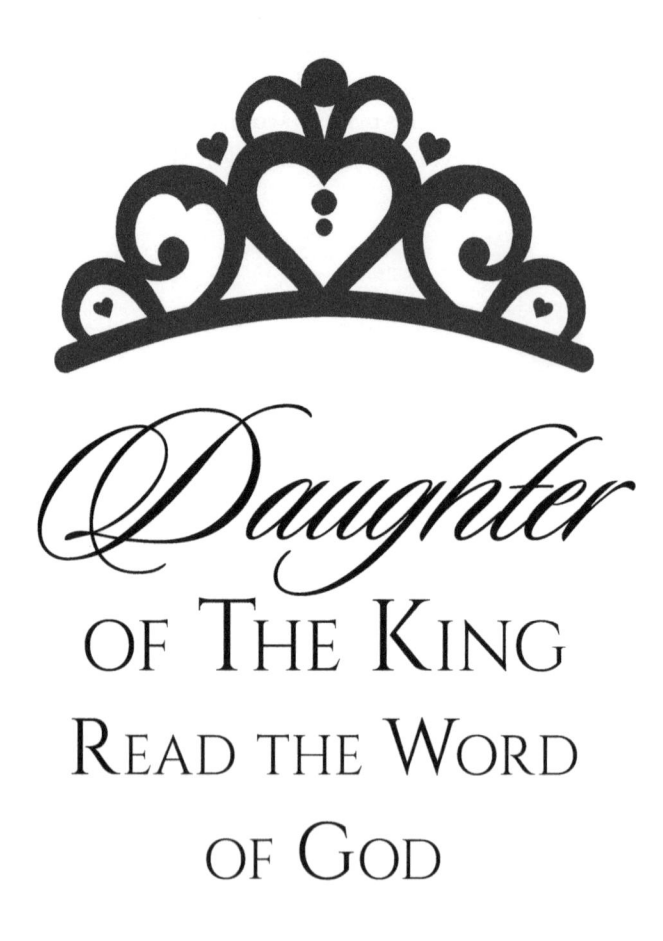

of The King
Read the Word
of God

DAY 31

A LIGHT TO MY PATH

Read Psalm 119:105-108

We all know that light will illuminate the darkness. Before salvation, you walked in darkness, apart from the light. As a believer, you now have God's Word which is truth, and the truth will bring light to your life where darkness once abided. Light in these verses refers to life and the Word of God is provided to give life. Reading God's word daily will provide a light that will brighten your day and guide you on your way. As you read and study God's word you will deepen your faith and grow spiritually.

Dear Heavenly Father,

Help me to read your word daily, understand what I read, and apply it to my life, so I can be both a hearer and doer of your Word. Amen!

Daughter

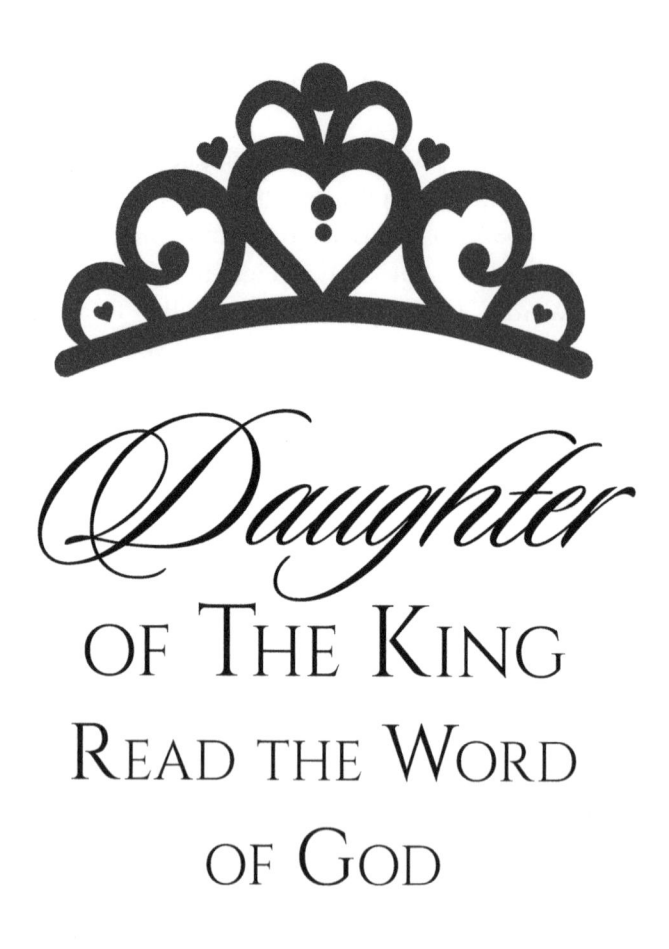

OF THE KING
READ THE WORD
OF GOD

DAY 32

LIVING BY GOD'S WORD

Read Matthew 4:1-11

Just as we eat physical food each day to provide the nutrients for our physical bodies, we also need spiritual nourishment for our spiritual bodies. Satan tried to tempt Jesus to turn stone into bread and Jesus replied, "It is written: 'Man shall not live on bread alone., but on every word that comes out of the mouth of God'." (Matthew 4:4) Reading God's Word each day will provide you with truths to live by and the spiritual nourishment you need to grow as a Christian. As you read God's Word, remember to make a note of what you learn, such as **S**ins to repent of, **I**nstructions to follow, **M**emorize this verse, **P**romises to keep, **L**ife application, and **E**ncouragement to remember. You can use the **"SIMPLE"** daily bible reading journal page located at the back of this devotional as a guide to assist you.

Dear Heavenly Father,
 Thank you for your word which gives me the spiritual nourishment I need to grow as your child. Amen.

Daughter
OF THE KING
READ THE WORD
OF GOD

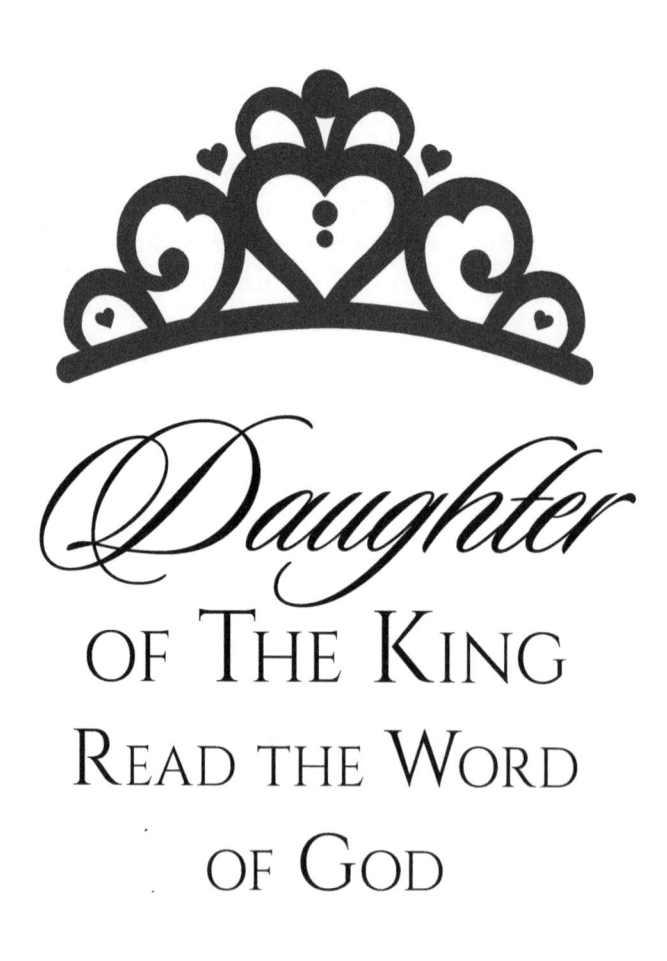

DAY 33

THE SWORD OF THE SPIRIT

Read Ephesians 6:10-17

As believers, we are given spiritual armor to dress up in daily. Each piece of armor has a specific purpose, but the full armor will protect us from the attacks from the enemy. The Bible is referred to as the sword of the spirit. This piece of armor will equip you with the truths you need to grow as a believer and should be used to assist you in taking negative and sinful thoughts captive. When you read God's Word each day, you will learn how to use your sword to defeat the enemy.

Dear Heavenly Father,

Thank you for providing spiritual armor to protect me from the attacks of the enemy. Remind me to suit up each day so I am prepared for spiritual battle. Amen!

Daughter

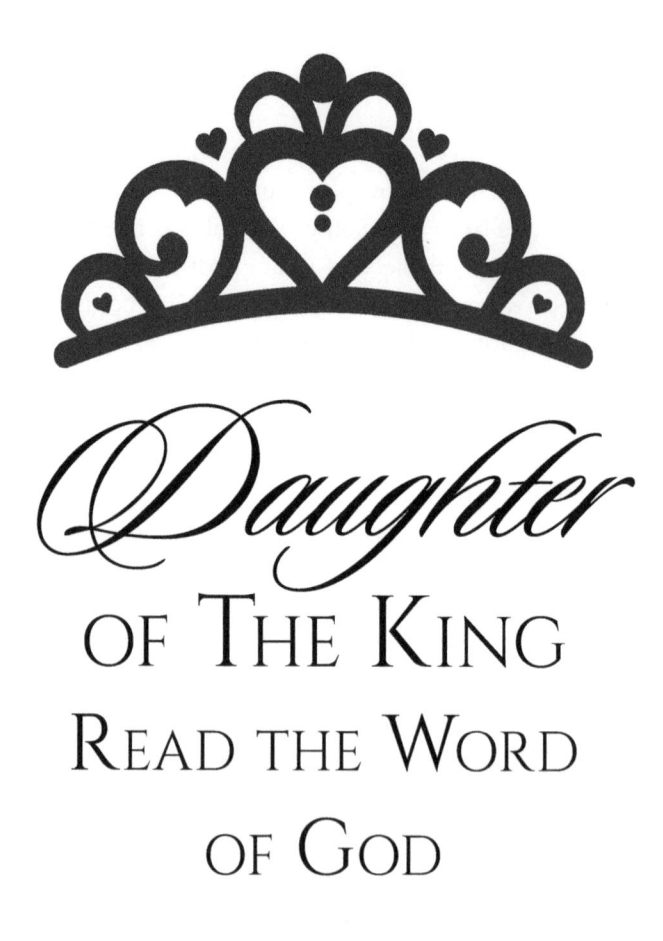

OF THE KING
READ THE WORD
OF GOD

DAY 34

STUDY GOD'S WORD

Read Second Timothy 2:14-18

Students study to prepare for a test to demonstrate the knowledge and understanding gained from the lessons they learned. Likewise, as believers, we must read and study God's word regularly. When we do, we will be equipped with truth and understanding, so we don't fall prey to false teaching. Through the power of the Holy Spirit, we will also be able to defend the Word when it is presented falsely. When we read God's word daily, we also gain discernment and knowledge on how to share God's Word with others.

Dear Heavenly Father,

    Thank you for the gift of Your word. Help me to read it every day, study it, and share the truth of Your word with others. Amen!

Daughter
of The King
Read the Word of God

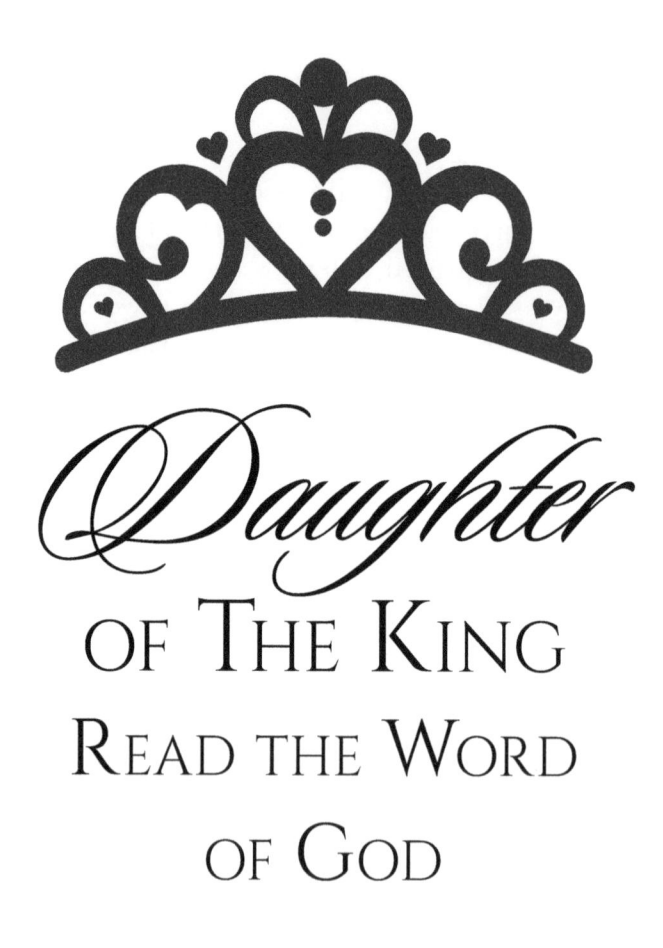

DAY 35

HIDE THE WORD OF GOD IN MY HEART

Read Psalm 119:9-11

When we know and understand the truth, we will obey it. These verses in Psalm 119 remind us that when we have God's word, which is truth, in our hearts, we will be reminded not to sin against God, especially when we are tempted to wander away. When we have God's Word hidden in our hearts, we will also desire to obey it. Reading God's Word daily will provide instructions to live by, pitfalls to avoid, and sins to repent of.

Dear Heavenly Father,

I'm so grateful that I can read your word and keep it in my heart as a reminder to live in true obedience to you. Amen!

MY COMMITMENT OF HOW I WILL APPLY THE SPIRITUAL DISCIPLINE OF READING GOD'S WORD.

In the space below, share how you will apply this spiritual discipline to your life.

_____

_____

_____

_____

_____

_____

_____

_____

_____

_____

_____

_____

_____

_____

Daughter
OF THE KING
PRAY ALWAYS

THE SPIRITUAL DISCIPLINE OF PRAYER

When we have a conversation with someone it is usually a two-way conversation. We say something and the other person responds. The spiritual discipline of prayer is talking with God, but also pausing to listen as He speaks to us. Prayer is not just a time to give God our list of things we want from Him, but it is a time to praise Him, thank Him, repent of sins, seek forgiveness, and pray for the needs of others.

When we present our request to God in prayer, we must remember God will respond in one of three ways, yes, no, or wait. Remember He has our best interest in mind, so regardless of his answer, we must always trust Him. Colossians 4:2 is a reminder for us, which says, "Devote yourselves to prayer, keeping alert in it with an attitude of thanksgiving." (NASB)

Daughter
OF THE KING
PRAY ALWAYS

DAY 36

JESUS TEACHES ME HOW TO PRAY

Read Matthew 6:9-13

Some people avoid praying when they are asked to pray because they feel they don't know how to pray, or they believe they are expected to pray like others. We can follow the guidelines Jesus provided when He taught us how to pray. We begin by acknowledging God as our Father and recognizing that He is holy. We seek his will and his provision. We ask for forgiveness of our sins and express our forgiveness to anyone who sinned against us. We seek protection and deliverance from the evil one. We end by acknowledging His kingdom, His power, and His glory.

Dear Heavenly Father,
    I am so thankful that I can spend time in prayer talking with you and that you will not only hear my prayers, but you will answer my requests in accordance with your will and plan for me. Amen!

Daughter
OF THE KING
Pray Always

DAY 37

PRAY AND CONFESS MY SINS

Read James 5:13-20

These verses in James 5 are an exhortation to us to pray and not just for ourselves, but to pray for those who are suffering and sick. It is also an exhortation to pray and confess our sins to one another and to pray for each other. This provides a great opportunity to establish accountability. Confessing our sins to one another allows us to have someone to hold us accountable for not continuously committing sin. We also can be prayer partners praying and interceding for one another. Remember when we pray, we don't only pray for ourselves, but we also can pray for the needs of others.

Dear Heavenly Father,
    Thank you for teaching me how to pray and confess my sins to a dear sister in Christ who would hold me accountable. Thank you for reminding me that I should not only spend time praying for me, but I should also pray for the needs of others. Amen!

Daughter

OF THE KING

PRAY ALWAYS

DAY 38

PRAY FOR MY ENEMIES

Read Matthew 5:43-48

How would you respond if you were asked, "Do you pray for your enemies?" It may sound crazy, but scripture instructs us to love our enemies and to pray for them. This is not an easy thing to do, but when you spend time in prayer, the Lord will provide the comfort and peace you need to not only love those who have hurt you, but to pray for them as well.

Dear Heavenly Father,

Teach me how to love and pray for those who seek to hurt and harm me. I pray for their salvation, that they may come to know you as Savior and acknowledge you as the Lord of their life. Amen!

Daughter
OF THE KING
PRAY ALWAYS

DAY 39

PRAY WITHOUT CEASING

Read First Thessalonians 5:16-18

The verses in First Thessalonians 5 provide specific instructions to follow when we pray. We should always be joyful, regardless of the circumstances we may be facing. We should pray without ceasing, which means we should never stop praying. Finally, when we pray, we should also be thankful whether things are going good or not going well. We are given these instructions to follow when we pray because it is God's will for us.

Dear Heavenly Father,
    Thank you for reminding me to pray always and to give thanks no matter how good or how bad my life circumstances may be. I choose to rejoice and give you thanks according to your will for me. Amen!

Daughter
OF THE KING
PRAY ALWAYS

DAY 40

GIVE THANKS IN ALL THINGS

Read Philippians 4:6-7

When we become fearful, we get fidgety and anxious. When this happens, we should remember that the Bible tells us not to be anxious about anything. As we pray with Thanksgiving, it's a time to submit our request to God, not only for ourselves, but also for others. He already knows what we need, and He will provide the peace that only He can give, and that peace will bring comfort to our hearts and our minds and will drive away fear and anxiety.

Dear Heavenly Father,
    Thank you for the peace and comfort you provide when I worry and become fearful. I'm so glad I can trust you in all things. Amen!

MY COMMITMENT OF HOW I WILL APPLY THE SPIRITUAL DISCIPLINE OF PRAYER.

In the space below, share how you will apply this spiritual discipline to your life.

_____

_____

_____

_____

_____

_____

_____

_____

_____

_____

_____

_____

_____

_____

Daughter
OF THE KING
MEDITATE ON GOD
AND HIS WORD

THE SPIRITUAL DISCIPLINE
OF MEDITATION

When we speak of meditation as believers, we are not referring to worldly meditation. The spiritual discipline of meditation is a dedicated time spent savoring the message of God's Word. When we read and meditate on scripture this provides insight into God's word and deepens our faith causing spiritual growth.

Colossians 3:16 is a wonderful reminder of how important the spiritual discipline of meditation is. This verse says, "Let the word of Christ richly dwell within you, with all wisdom, teaching and admonishing one another with psalms, hymns, *and* spiritual songs, singing with thankfulness in your hearts to God." (NASB)

Daughter
of The King
Meditate on God
and His Word

DAY 41

MEDITATE ON GOD'S WORD

Read Joshua 1:7-8

Joshua 1:7-8 provides encouragement to meditate regularly on God's Word and to obey "all" that is written in it. This means we must do more than just read a verse or two periodically. We should read, meditate "ponder and think" on what we read, and do what God's Word says to do. There is a reward for our obedience. When we spend time meditating on God's Word and obeying God, we will prosper and have good success.

Dear Heavenly Father,

Thank you for the guidance to spend time meditating on your word and the importance of obeying all that you ask me to do. Amen!

Daughter of The King
Meditate on God and His Word

DAY 42

MEDITATE DAY AND NIGHT

Read Psalm 1:1-2

Psalm 1:1-2 reminds us that the Word of God will never depart from us. Therefore, we should meditate on it day and night and do everything that is written in it. If God's word is constantly leading and guiding us, then rightfully so, we should meditate on it. As we meditate on his word, God will speak to our hearts and provide the wisdom and guidance we need to obey him. There is a promise in these verses as well, which says, if you meditate regularly on God's Word and obey it, then we will be prosperous and have success, which is similar to the verses we read in Joshua 1:7-8. Let's be clear, this is not a prosperity message. God, and only God, knows the plans he has for our lives. But if you want God's blessing, it is important to obey His word.

Dear Heavenly Father,
    Thank you for teaching me the importance of spending time meditating and obeying your word. I choose to follow your instructions. Amen!

Daughter
of The King
Meditate on God and His Word

DAY 43

MEDITATE ON THESE THINGS

Read Philippians 4:8-9

As a believer, Satan will always try to get us to worry, be fearful, and cause us to think on things contrary to God's word. Because the Holy Spirit lives in us, he will provide what we need to control our thoughts. These verses in Philippians share specific attributes we should meditate on. We are encouraged to think on things that are always truthful, honorable, just, right, pure, lovely, and admirable. Why? Because all these things are praiseworthy to God. When we think on these things the peace of God will always be with us.

Dear Heavenly Father,
   Help me to keep my mind and thoughts on you, your word, and the things that are praiseworthy. Amen!

Daughter of The King

Meditate on God and His Word

DAY 44

MEDITATE ON GOD'S CREATION AND BLESSINGS

Read Psalm 143:5-6

Have you ever stopped and meditated on your past, thinking about good memories and some memories that may not be so good? These verses encourage us to meditate on all that God has done. So stop, look around at God's creation; the sky, clouds, sun, moon, stars, flowers, trees, birds and, there's so much more. When you do, you will be amazed at the beauty in all that God has done. Take a moment to meditate about your life, think about where you were before you were saved and where you are now. Then you will cherish the blessing of how God created you and where God has brought you from to where you are today.

Dear Heavenly Father,

Thank you for your beautiful creation in our world, how you created me and for all the blessings that you have given to me. Amen!

Daughter
of The King
Meditate on God and His Word

DAY 45

MEDITATE ON GOD'S PRECEPTS

Read Psalm 119:12-16

A precept is a command or a principle and the Bible is full of them. These five verses in Psalm 119 remind us that we should spend time meditating on God's commands and we should also memorize them, so they are hidden in our heart. When we hide God's word in our hearts, they are not literally hidden where we can't find them, but they are stored away and the Holy Spirit, our Comforter will remind us of the specific verse(s) at just the right time. So, when we meditate on God's precepts we are filling our hearts with more of God's Word.

Dear Heavenly Father,
    Thank you for the guidance to spend time meditating on your word and the importance of obeying all that you ask me to do. I will not forget your word but will keep it always in my heart. Amen!

Daughter
of The King
Meditate on God and His Word

MY COMMITMENT OF HOW I WILL APPLY THE SPIRITUAL DISCIPLINE OF MEDITATION.

In the space below, share how you will apply this spiritual discipline to your life.

_____

_____

_____

_____

_____

_____

_____

_____

_____

_____

_____

_____

_____

_____

Daughter
of The King
Spend Time Fasting

THE SPIRITUAL DISCIPLINE OF FASTING

There are many examples of fasting in the bible. Some examples include individuals who have fasted and examples of groups of people who fasted. The spiritual discipline of fasting includes abstaining from food for spiritual purposes. When you fast, scripture encourages us to do it in secret, which means we do not have to let everyone know we are fasting.

Matthew 6:17-18 says, "But as for you, when you fast, anoint your head and wash your face, so that your fasting will not be noticed by people but by your Father who is in secret; and your Father who sees what is done in secret will reward you." (NASB)

Daughter
of The King
Spend Time Fasting

DAY 46

HOW WE SHOULD FAST

Read Matthew 6:16-18

Fasting is one of the spiritual disciplines that it's not practice regularly by Christians. It may be because they don't know how to fast, or they may not understand what fasting is. The verses in Matthew 6 provided clear instructions for those living in that time. But there is one clear instruction we should follow when we fast, which is, when we fast, we don't have to broadcast it to everyone.

Another thing we must remember is that fasting is personal between us and God. So, when we fast, we are usually abstaining from something and using that time to spend reading God's word and praying.

Dear Heavenly Father,
  Thank you for the wisdom and instruction on how to fast and how to use that time as a personal time between me and You. Amen!

Daughter
OF THE KING
SPEND TIME FASTING

DAY 47

A BIBLICAL ILLUSTRATION OF FASTING - MOSES

Read Deuteronomy 9:7-29

God chose Moses to lead the children of Israel from Egypt to the promise land. However, many of them were rebellious and complained regularly. When God called Moses to the mountain to give him the ten commandments Moses fasted 40 days and nights interceding on behalf of the children of Israel. Their disobedience and rebellion displeased the Lord and he wanted to destroy them. In verses 26 -29, we see that Moses interceded asking God to not destroy them since He had redeemed them and promised to bring them to the land filled with milk and honey. From this illustration we can learn that we can fast to intercede on the behalf of others.

Dear Heavenly Father,
  Thank you for the reminder that I can fast and intercede on behalf of others. Amen!

Daughter
of The King
Spend Time Fasting

DAY 48

A BIBLICAL ILLUSTRATION OF FASTING - ESTHER

Read Esther 4-6

When the news spread in Susa that all the Jews would be killed, Mordecai appealed to Queen Esther for help. Esther reminded him that she could not approach the King unless she was summoned. Esther asked Mordecai to assemble all the people in Susa and have everyone abstain from food and water and to pray and fast for three days and night. There are many occasions where a group of believers or the church will join together and fast and pray seeking directions and guidance from the Lord. When you fast with a group remember to be committed and follow the instructions of the fast.

Dear Heavenly Father,
   Thank you for the opportunity to join with other believers to fast and pray for your guidance in specific matters. May we always be true to adhere to your response. Amen!

Daughter
of The King
Spend Time Fasting

DAY 49

A BIBLICAL ILLUSTRATION OF FASTING - DANIEL

Read Daniel 10-12

Daniel fasted partially for three weeks abstaining only from food as he sought the wisdom and guidance of God. There are many individuals and churches that participate in what is referred to as the Daniel fast, where for twenty-one days they abstain from meat, dairy, alcohol, and other rich foods. During this partial fast, they eat vegetables and water as they spend time in fervent and focused prayer and reading God's Word. No matter whether you do a full or partial fast, remember the purpose of fasting is to spend dedicated time with God in prayer and reading His word.

Dear Heavenly Father,

I am committed to fast and pray to draw closer to you, to present my requests to you, and to listen as you respond and provide instructions and guidance. Amen!

Daughter
of The King
Spend Time Fasting

DAY 50

A BIBLICAL ILLUSTRATION OF FASTING - JESUS

Read Luke 4:1-13

While Jesus was in the wilderness for 40 days and nights he fasted during this time. He did not eat anything. While in the wilderness, Satan tempted him to turn from serving God and to serve him. The lesson we can learn from Jesus' fast is that we may be tempted when we are fasting, but we are also strengthened as we devote ourselves to reading God's Word and having a time of focused and fervent prayer. If we are committed to growing spiritually, we will remain true to completing the time of fasting successfully.

Dear Heavenly Father,

Help me to remain committed to spending time reading your word and praying during my time of fasting, so I can hear from you. Deliver me from the temptations I may experience during fasting, so I may draw closer to you. Amen!

MY COMMITMENT OF HOW I WILL APPLY THE SPIRITUAL DISCIPLINE OF FASTING.

In the space below, share how you will apply this spiritual discipline to your life.

_____

_____

_____

_____

_____

_____

_____

_____

_____

_____

_____

_____

_____

_____

Daughter
of The King
Spend Time in Solitude with God

THE SPIRITUAL DISCIPLINE OF SOLITUDE

The spiritual discipline of solitude includes finding a quiet place where there are no distractions where we can spend time praying and listening to God. A quiet place doesn't always have to be a place in your home, you can also go for a walk, or have this quiet time while driving. The importance of having a time of solitude is being silent before the Lord, so we can hear as he speaks.

Psalm 23:1-3 is a beautiful example of the spiritual discipline of solitude, which says, "The Lord is my shepherd, I will not be in need. He lets me lie down in green pastures; He leads me beside quiet waters. He restores my soul; He guides me in the paths of righteousness. For the sake of His name." (NASB)

Daughter
OF THE KING
SPEND TIME IN SOLITUDE WITH GOD

DAY 51

A TIME OF SOLITUDE – FIND A QUIET PLACE

Read Matthew 14:22-23

When Jesus heard about the death of John the Baptist, he went to a quiet place to be alone. There are times in your life when you will need a time of solitude, and it may not always be time to grieve. Remember solitude is a time where you can be still before the Lord with no interruptions or distractions. When you need time for solitude, that dedicated time alone with God, do what Jesus did, and find a quiet place to be alone with God.

Dear Heavenly Father,

Thank you for the reminder that I can make time to spend alone with you for a time of solitude away from the daily distractions. Amen!

Daughter
of The King
Spend Time in Solitude with God

DAY 52

A TIME OF SOLITUDE – USE YOUR TIME WISELY

Read Matthew 4:1-11

Jesus spent 40 days and 40 nights in the wilderness. During that time, he was tempted several times by Satan. Jesus responded to each temptation with the word of God. The lesson we can learn from Jesus is use our time of solitude wisely. We can do this by quietly reading and memorizing scripture. During our time of solitude, we can expect temptations to come in the form of distractions, wandering thoughts, text, or phone calls. Another lesson we can learn is to respond to temptations like Jesus did by responding with God's word.

Dear Heavenly Father,
   Thank you for reminding me that during my time of solitude I can pray and read your word, which will equip and prepare me to respond appropriately to interruptions and distractions. Amen!

Daughter
of The King
Spend Time in Solitude with God

DAY 53

A TIME OF SOLITUDE – INCLUDE A TIME OF REST

Read Mark 6:30-31

Earlier in Mark 6, Jesus sent his disciples out with specific ministry assignments. When they returned, Jesus told them to go to a secluded place to rest. We live in a society where we are always on the go. There is so much to be done and so little time to do it. Jesus knew the importance of getting rest. If a time to rest was important to Jesus, it needs to be important to us as well. So, when you plan a time of solitude, include the time to also rest.

Dear Heavenly Father,

Thank you that I can spend the time of solitude as a time to rest. Amen!

Daughter
of The King
Spend Time in Solitude with God

DAY 54

A TIME OF SOLITUDE – EXPECT TO MEET GOD

Read Luke 6:12-16

Before Jesus chose the 12 apostles, he spent all night in prayer. While scripture does not specifically point this out, it may be that he was praying for guidance from the Father on which of the group of disciples should He select as the twelve Apostles. Jesus knew in his time of solitude that the Father would meet him there. When we have important decisions to make, we spend time in prayer seeking wisdom and guidance from the Lord. When we enter our time of prayerful solitude, we shouldn't enter hoping God will meet us there, we should enter expecting to meet God there.

Dear Heavenly Father,

I'm so grateful that during my time of solitude I know that you will be there with me because you promised that you would never leave or forsake me. Amen!

Daughter
of The King
Spend Time in Solitude with God

DAY 55

A TIME OF SOLITUDE – TIME TO TALK TO GOD

Read Matthew 26:36-46

When Jesus went to pray in the garden of Gethsemane, He wanted to talk to His Father. He knew what he would face in the days ahead. The verses in Matthew 26 states he told his disciples, "My soul is deeply grieved." Jesus knew that his time in prayer with the Father would bring the comfort he needed to endure and face the cross. When we are overwhelmed with a heavy burden, we can get alone in a time of silent solitude and talk to God. Remember, scripture reminds us to cast all our cares on Him because He cares for us. (First Peter 5:7, NASB)

Dear Heavenly Father,
    I am so thankful that during my time of silent solitude I can talk to you and share all my cares and concerns. Amen!

MY COMMITMENT OF HOW I WILL APPLY THE SPIRITUAL DISCIPLINE OF SOLITUDE.

In the space below, share how you will apply this spiritual discipline to your life.

_____

_____

_____

_____

_____

_____

_____

_____

_____

_____

_____

_____

_____

_____

Daughter
OF THE KING
WORSHIP THE LORD

THE SPIRITUAL DISCIPLINE OF WORSHIP

Worship is a dedicated time we spend praising God. Worship is not only done in singing but we can worship the Lord during our prayer time, by sharing our testimony of when we came to faith in Christ, and by living our life in a manner that pleases and glorify God. The spiritual discipline of worship is also done with other believers, as we come together to worship the Lord corporately.

John 4:23 reminds of the need for the spiritual discipline of worship. This verse says, "But a time is coming, and even now has arrived, when the true worshipers will worship the Father in spirit and truth; for such people the Father seeks to be His worshipers." (NASB)

Daughter
of The King
Worship the Lord

DAY 56

LIFT YOUR HANDS IN WORSHIP TO THE LORD

Read Psalm 63:1-4

There are many scriptures that discuss praise and worship to God. This Psalm is written by David praising God for his strength, faithful love, and his glory. When you worship God while singing do you lift your hands? Lifting our hands to the Lord is a sign of surrendering our all to him and acknowledging that we are directing our praise to God and God alone. Because he is worthy of praise, we should never be ashamed or hesitate to lift our hands in worship to the Lord.

Dear Heavenly Father,

I lift my hands in adoration and praise as I worship you because you are worthy of all my praise. Amen!

Daughter
of The King
Worship the Lord

DAY 57

WORSHIP OUR GREAT GOD

Read Psalm 95:1-3

The Book of Psalms is full of songs of worship to God. The first three verses in Psalms 95 express our worship of God, acknowledging how good and how great He is. When we worship God, whether in prayer, song, or testimony, we should express how good he is and the great things he has done. Remember, our worship is to God and no one else. Worship is also a time to give him thanks for all that He has done.

Dear Heavenly Father,
    Thank you for the many blessings you have given to me, and all you have done. I thank you for my salvation and for the opportunity to worship and praise you. Amen!

Daughter
OF THE KING
WORSHIP THE LORD

DAY 58

WORSHIP AND BOW DOWN BEFORE THE LORD

Read Psalm 95:6-7

Many of the worship choruses you hear sung today include lyrics from the Bible. Psalms 95:6-7 is just one of those worship songs. Although we are usually standing during our time of corporate worship at church, in our hearts we are bowing before the Lord as sing in adoration and praise to our God. When we bow before the Lord, we acknowledge His Holiness and worthiness of receiving worship, because He is God!

Dear Heavenly Father,
    I bow before you in adoration and praise of who you are, and I worship you with all that I am. Amen!

Daughter
OF THE KING
WORSHIP THE LORD

DAY 59

A CALL TO PRAISE AND WORSHIP

Read Psalm 150

Psalm 150 is a great call to praise and worship our great God. It's a reminder that we should praise Him wherever we are, with many instruments, with dancing, and with our mouths. No matter the circumstances we may face, we should never forsake having the time to worship and praise our God. Let everything that hath breath, praise the Lord.

Dear Heavenly Father,

I enjoy worshipping and praising you with my voice, my hands, and with all my heart. As long as I live, I will give you my worship. Amen!

Daughter
of The King
Worship the Lord

DAY 60

JOIN WITH THE ANGELS AND WORSHIP GOD

Read Revelations 7:9-12

When we get to heaven, we will join with a multitude of other believers from every nation, every tongue, and every tribe for a time of worshipping our God throughout eternity. We will join with the angels saying, "Blessing, glory, wisdom, thanksgiving, honor, power, and might belong to our God, forever and ever! You don't have to wait to get to heaven to worship God. Remember you can have your time of personal worship and a time of corporate worship at church with your brothers and sisters in Christ. Exalt the Lord, our God, and worship Him every day!

Dear Heavenly Father,
    I worship you because of who you are. You are Holy, Holy God! Amen!

MY COMMITMENT OF HOW I WILL APPLY THE SPIRITUAL DISCIPLINE OF WORSHIP.

In the space below, share how you will apply this spiritual discipline to your life.

_____

_____

_____

_____

_____

_____

_____

_____

_____

_____

_____

_____

DAILY BIBLE READING JOURNAL

Scripture Reading: _____

After reading, here's what I learned:

Sins to forsake: _____
_____
_____
_____

Instructions to follow: _____
_____
_____
_____

Memorize this verse: _____
_____
_____
_____

Promise to keep: _____
_____
_____
_____

Life application: _____
_____
_____
_____

Encouragement to remember: _____
_____
_____
_____

A Daily Devotional for Daughters of The King

DAILY BIBLE READING JOURNAL
(EXAMPLE)

Scripture Reading: _____John 3:16-21_____

After reading, here's what I learned:

Sins to forsake: Any disbelief I have regarding the Bible and who God is, because God is real, and his word is truth. (v.16 &18)

Instructions to follow: Whoever does what is true comes to the light, so that it may be clearly seen that his works have been carried out in God. (v.21)

Memorize this verse: For God so loved the world, that he gave his only Son, that whoever believes in him should not perish, but have eternal life. (v.16)

Promise to keep: Whoever believes in him (God) is not condemned. (V.18a)

Life application: Whoever believes in him (God) should not perish, but have eternal life. (v.16)

Encouragement to remember: God did not send his Son into the world to condemn the world, but that the world might be saved through him. (v. 17)

A Daily Devotional for Daughters of The King

Milton Keynes UK
Ingram Content Group UK Ltd.
UKHW010639270324
440147UK00012B/243/J